Everything You Need to Know About

The Dangers of Tattooing and Body Piercing

Tattooing is often a proud symbol of rebellion for individualists.

Everything You Need to Know About The Dangers of Tattooing and Body Piercing

Laura Reybold

The Rosen Publishing Group, Inc.
New York

The author wishes to thank Inferno Body Piercing and Olde City Tattoo for their assistance with this book.

Published in 1996, 1998, 2001 by The Rosen Publishing Group, Inc.
29 East 21st Street, New York, NY 10010

Revised Edition 2001

Library of Congress Cataloging-in-Publication Data

Reybold, Laura.
Everything you need to know about the dangers of tattooing and body piercing / Laura Reybold
p. cm.—(The Need to Know Library)
Includes bibliographical references and index.
Summary: Presents a history of body piercing and tattooing before discussing the risks and consequences involved.
ISBN 0-8239-3469-1
1. Body piercing—Health aspects—Juvenile literature. 2. Tattooing—Health aspects—Juvenile literature. [1. Body piercing. 2. Tattooing.] I. Title II. The Need to Know Library (New York, N.Y.)
RD119.5N82R48 1998
617.9'5—dc20

95-20227

Manufactured in the United States of America

Contents

Introduction

Once associated with those on the fringes of society—slaves, ex-convicts, pirates, sailors, bikers, gang members, and freak show performers—tattoos and body piercings have entered the mainstream. Such popular and successful stars as Drew Barrymore, Johnny Depp, Dennis Rodman, Michael Jordan, Elle MacPherson, Steven Tyler, Cher, and Madonna have adopted these underground styles and proudly flaunt their body decorations. Tattoos and piercings are now even being sported by some businesspeople, lawyers, and politicians. The number of tattoo parlors nationwide has jumped from 300 to over 4,000 in the last twenty years. It is estimated that more than 10 million Americans have at least one tattoo.

Anyone who gets tattooed or pierced is sharing in an ancient tradition of body art. For centuries, people have decorated their bodies and faces with tattoos and piercings in many different ways, depending on their culture, the time they lived in, and their individual beliefs. Tattoos and body piercings may be performed for spiritual or religious reasons; to celebrate an important stage, event, or person in one's life; to show one's social status; to create romantic attraction; to "reclaim" one's body following some kind of trauma; or simply to be different from everyone else. Today, many people are drawn to body art simply because it is a fashion trend.

Are you considering getting a tattoo or a piercing? If so, you need to think seriously about your decision. Tattoos and piercings will leave permanent marks on your body. While fashion trends come and go, your tattoo or piercing may be with you forever.

Also, getting a tattoo or body piercing poses serious health risks. Both procedures puncture your skin, leaving your body vulnerable to infections and diseases. You can reduce the risk of infection and disease by having a tattoo or piercing performed by a professional in a sanitary environment and by maintaining proper hygiene while the site heals. However, any tattoo or piercing can cause physical discomfort or result in infection, even if you take proper care of it.

This book will alert you to the risks and consequences of getting a tattoo or piercing. You will learn how tattoos and piercings should be performed and

Tattooing has been popularized by celebrities such as actor Johnny Depp, actor Drew Barrymore (that's her back in the center photo), and athlete Dennis Rodman.

the safety precautions you should take to minimize health risks. It will also discuss removal treatments for those who want to get rid of their tattoos or piercings. Finally, it will present various ways to help you feel part of the body-art trend without permanently affecting your body.

Tattoos and piercings can be a lifetime commitment. It is important to know the facts and risks involved. Making a safe and informed decision will satisfy you both now and in the future.

Chapter 1

The History and Process of Tattooing

Tattooing is a traditional art form practiced by many cultures in many societies. It is a permanent method of decorating the body, performed by puncturing the surface of the skin with a sharp tool or needle and inserting colored inks or dyes into the second layer of skin. The word "tattoo" comes from the Tahitian word *tatau*, which means to knock, strike, or mark something. Tattoos have meant many different things to many different cultures. Tattoos have been used to express religious devotion; to celebrate a right of passage; to demonstrate tolerance of pain; to indicate someone's membership in a tribe, family, gang, or military unit; to identify prisoners; and to rebel against mainstream society. Many of the

young people who are getting tattoos feel that tattooing is a way to gain control over the only aspect of
their lives they are allowed to control: their bodies.

It seems that tattooing began in Egypt sometime
between 4,000 and 2,000 BC. From Egypt, the art
traveled throughout the world, spreading to Greece,
Rome, Persia, China, Japan, the Pacific Islands, and New
Zealand. It is possible that Native Americans learned
the art of tattooing from migrating Polynesians. There
is evidence that Celtic tribes and invading Vikings
introduced tattooing to Britain before the "barbaric
practice" was banned in AD 787 by Pope Adrian I.

After disappearing for centuries, tattooing was
reintroduced to Britain and the rest of Europe in 1691
following the English explorer William Dampier's
return from his voyage to the South Seas. During his
trip, Dampier had met a man whose body was entirely
covered in tattoos and brought him back to England in
order to put him on display. Eighty years later,
another English explorer, Captain Cook, also brought
back with him a completely tattooed Polynesian man.
When these men were shown around London, they
created such a sensation that the noble classes began
to get small tattoos of their own. This revived the art
of tattooing in the Western world.

Soon, dukes and kings and even Sir Winston
Churchill's mother were lining up to get tattoos.

Because they were very expensive, tattoos remained an art form for the elite. In 1891, however, Samuel O'Reilly patented the first electric tattoo machine. The price of tattoos quickly dropped, and they became more affordable to the common man and woman. Now that almost anyone could get a tattoo, the upper classes lost interest and tattoos soon became associated with the lower classes.

Tattooing in the United States

By 1897, tattooing had reached the United States, where tattooed people immediately became circus sideshow attractions. Over the next fifty years, the number of tattooed individuals in the United States rose steadily. Military men had tattoos representing the type or location of their service, young lovers declared their eternal love through tattoos, and devoted sons proudly displayed "Mom" on their arms. Tattoo artists expanded the selection of designs, known as flash, displayed on the walls of their tattoo parlors. Flash was sold in sets that could be legally reproduced onto stencils and bodies. Flash is still sold in the same manner today.

Today in the United States, tattooing is against the law in some communities, mainly because of a concern about the possible spread of disease and infection through the use of contaminated needles and pigments. In other places, it is restricted to persons at least eighteen years of age. Where tattooing is legal, however, there is little or no government regulation of tattoo artists and their facilities. This means that there may be unscrupulous or incompetent tattooists, called scratchers, who do not follow important safety precautions when tattooing their clients. Tattooing opens your body to potential infection, disease, and scarring. For this reason, it's important to safeguard your health by knowing what to expect from the tattoo process.

How Is Tattooing Done?

A responsible tattoo artist first discusses the design and placement of the tattoo with his or her client and answers any questions the client may have. He or she should also be prepared to show the client the studio's facilities and sterilization equipment, if requested.

When the client is ready, the tattooist starts by making a stencil, or tracing, of the design. The design can be altered or redone if the client isn't satisfied with it. The stencil is then placed on the client's skin, where it leaves behind a replica of the design. The tattooist follows the outline with a device called an outliner, which uses needles to inject ink into the skin. There may be a lot of bleeding during this procedure.

A professional tattoo artist should be willing to answer a client's questions and address concerns about safety.

Next, the tattoo artist shades in and colors the design using a shader. When the tattoo is complete, the tattoo artist should provide a pamphlet with instructions on how to care for the new tattoo.

Most tattoo artists still use an electric machine based on the original invented by Samuel O'Reilly. Over the years, many changes and improvements have been made to O'Reilly's machine. In addition, in recent years, many refinements have made the tattooing process safer and more hygienic than in the past. An autoclave, which sterilizes equipment using steam pressure, is an essential part of any responsible tattoo studio. All needles and equipment must be properly sterilized in the autoclave. Immersing needles in boiling water or rubbing them with disinfectant will not kill all viruses or bacteria. If a tattooist does not adequately sterilize equipment, you risk contracting bacterial and viral infections. Hepatitis can be transmitted through the use of unsterilized needles, as can the herpes simplex virus, or even HIV (human immunodeficiency virus), the virus that causes AIDS (acquired immuno-deficiency syndrome). A tattoo artist should also wear surgical gloves to ensure proper hygiene.

Thus far, there have been no medical reports of HIV infection from professional tattooing. Yet doctors warn that transmission of HIV through unsafe tattooing practices is possible and that people should be careful to protect themselves.

Several self-regulating associations of tattoo artists strive to make tattooing safe. One such group is the Alliance of Professional Tattooists, Inc. (APT). APT holds lectures to update tattoo artists on information about sterilization techniques and distributes guidelines for tattooists regarding disease control. If you decide to get a tattoo, use a studio that belongs to APT or to the National Tattoo Association (NTA).

Scarification

In addition to tattoos, scarification is another ancient and more extreme form of body marking that is

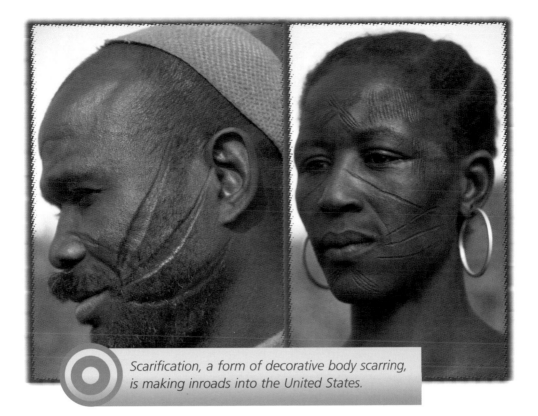

Scarification, a form of decorative body scarring, is making inroads into the United States.

becoming more and more popular in the United States. Scarification is the intentional creation of decorative scars on one's body. Scarification has been most often practiced in Africa and among the native people of Australia and New Guinea. The practice has made its way to the United States in recent years and is one of the latest trends among those in the hardcore "body art" community. Studies have shown that a large percentage of those who scar their skin are young people who have suffered some form of abuse and are seeking to reclaim control over their bodies.

There are two basic types of scarification: cutting and branding. Cutting is a slicing of the skin with a thin blade that results in a permanent scar. The skin is cut in such a way that the resulting scar will resemble a certain symbol, shape, word, or pattern. Sometimes, the fresh wound is rubbed with ink as well, leaving a colored scar. Those who desire a more raised scar often rub an irritant into the fresh wound, such as ash, red wine vinegar, or clay.

Branding is a form of scarification in which the skin is burned by contact with some heated material, usually metal, leaving a scar in some desired pattern or shape. These procedures are offered by many reputable tattoo and piercing parlors, but, unfortunately, many people choose to scar themselves or have their unqualified friends help them. You should never try to scar yourself or allow an amateur to do it to you.

As with tattooing and piercing, the main dangers of scarification—especially if performed by an amateur in an unsafe and unsterile environment—are blood-borne infections such as HIV, hepatitis B and C, syphilis, and potentially deadly staph and strep infections. Scarification can also result in skin color changes around the scar and the development of keloids—raised, bumpy scars. As with tattooing and piercing, all equipment used for scarification should be properly sterilized, and the procedure should be carried out by a professional who is wearing surgical gloves and working in a sanitary environment.

Chapter 2

The History and Process of Body Piercing

The history of body piercing is not as well documented as that of tattooing. But the practice of piercing a hole through the skin and inserting a piece of metal, bone, shell, ivory, or glass to wear as jewelry has been around for thousands of years. The face is the most common area to pierce because of its soft tissue. Throughout history and across many cultures, however, many other body parts have been pierced.

Ear, nose, and lip ornaments have been found in the burial sites of the Incas of Peru and the Aztecs and Maya of Mexico, and in the graves of central Asian and Mediterranean peoples. Body piercing was often associated with royalty and was a sign of courage and strength. Egyptian pharaohs pierced their navels to demonstrate their nobility, while a peasant found with a navel ring would be executed. Roman soldiers pierced their nipples as a sign of bravery and loyalty to the emperor, and the rings also served to hold their cloaks in place. Aztec and Mayan high priests pierced their tongues in order to speak to their gods. Among the Tlingit peoples of southeast Alaska, a nose piercing was thought to be a status symbol for both men and women. In many cultures, pierced ears showed that someone was wealthy. Sometimes, piercing was part of a ceremony marking a coming of age, change in social status, or beginning of a term of public office. Many sailors used to pierce their ears, thinking that it gave them better eyesight.

Body piercing continues to be practiced worldwide on men, women, and children. In the United States, piercing has steadily grown in popularity since the beginning of the twentieth century, when earrings for women first began to be popular. Ear piercing is the most common form of piercing in the United States today and has become more mainstream for men and women of all ages than it once was. In the 1980s, it became common for women and men to have multiple piercings in their ears. The 1990s brought a whole new array of body piercings. Nose, eyebrow, lip, tongue, cheek, belly button or navel, and septum (the part of

Many have pierced their ears for years, but piercing other parts of the body is gaining popularity in the United States.

the nose that separates the two nostrils) piercings all have become a new fashion statement.

Like all fashion statements, piercings will probably fall out of style eventually. But, unlike a pair of jeans, your body piercing can't be stored away in the attic. It's a part of your body. Since piercing can have permanent effects, it may be worth considering alternatives, such as jewelry for your nose, navel, or ears that only appears to be attached through a piercing.

Little government regulation applies to body piercing. Few local governments actively monitor piercing establishments. For that reason, it is essential that you guard your own health.

The Process of Piercing

All piercings should be performed by a professional—never by someone who is not specially trained. Important nerve tissue, muscle tissue, and organs can suffer permanent injury if a piercing is performed improperly.

It is essential that the equipment be sterilized. Even disposable needles should be sterilized. It is possible to contract HIV, hepatitis B and C, tuberculosis, syphilis, tetanus, and other bloodborne diseases from an unsterilized needle. Contracting any of these diseases is dangerous. But the risk of contracting HIV from an unsterilized needle is the greatest risk because HIV causes AIDS, which is nearly always fatal. There is no known cure for AIDS. For that reason, an autoclave should be standard equipment in every piercing studio. Never get pierced at a studio without one.

Piercings of various body parts are performed differently. A piercing gun should not be used for any kind of piercing, even for an ear piercing, because its needle cannot be sterilized, it hurts more than a piercing needle, and it inserts cheap jewelry that may cause infection or allergies. Most piercings are performed with a specially designed needle. Topical anesthesia is sometimes used, depending on the location of the piercing, but usually there is nothing to numb the pain.

 Dots are drawn to help guide where a piercer will place the needle that enters and leaves the client's flesh.

Some piercings, including navel piercings, are performed with the use of a surgical clamp. The piercer cleans the area with a disinfectant, such as rubbing alcohol, and draws two dots on the area to be pierced. One dot marks the spot where the needle will enter the body, the other where the needle will exit. The area to be pierced is then clamped, pulling the skin to be pierced away from the rest of the body. This eliminates the possibility of accidentally piercing vital body tissue. Nose piercings, like most facial piercings, are performed with a needle. Again, dots are made at the points where the needle should enter and exit. The piercer then pushes the needle through the flesh.

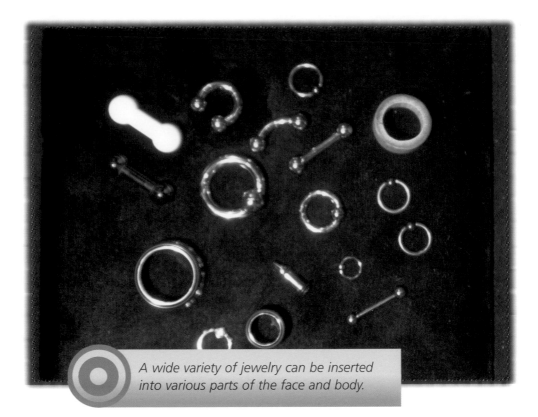

A wide variety of jewelry can be inserted into various parts of the face and body.

Specially designed jewelry is inserted in all piercings. Earrings are not suitable for most piercings other than those in the ears. Doug Malloy and Jim Ward, who are credited with being the popularizers of modern piercing, designed a whole line of body jewelry in the 1970s. More recently, the fashion designer Jean-Paul Gaultier has created jewelry for pierced bodies, including chains that hang between a pierced ear and nose. Ring-shaped jewelry is inserted in navel piercings. Other piercings can have either ring or stud-type jewelry inserted. Body jewelry is available in different sizes (gauges) that are appropriate for certain piercings.

Body jewelry should always be composed of fourteen-karat gold, surgical steel, or titanium. Other metals that are frequently used for jewelry making, including sterling silver, nickel, and copper, should never be inserted in a fresh piercing. These metals do not promote healing and may even cause an infection. Once the piercing is healed, you can use acrylic, pyrex, plastic, and wood jewelry.

It is also possible for a person to have an allergic reaction to any kind of metal jewelry, including those made of gold or surgical steel. If this is the case, your body is sensitive to foreign objects and is not well suited to piercing. If you are aware of having any allergies to metal, it is probably best to avoid piercing.

Extreme Piercing: Implants

As radical as nose, tongue, navel, and eyebrow piercings may seem (especially to your parents, teachers, and boss), there is always a new frontier opening up, redefining the border between the familiar and the shocking. The world of body art is no different. In the last few years, an extreme form of "body modification" has emerged in the United States: implants.

There are three main types of implants currently available: bead, 3-D art, and transdermal implants. Beading involves the insertion of small beads under the skin to create a variety of possible shapes, symbols, and designs. 3-D art implants are similar to bead implants but involve objects such as rings, crosses, balls, and barbells. Transdermal implants, unlike bead and 3-D art implants, do not lie entirely under the surface of the skin. One end passes through the skin while the other end remains sticking out. Some transdermal implants include a "metal mohawk" (a row of metal spikes running along the top of the skull), devil horns (like the ones the musician Enigma wears), and beads that appear on the surface of the skin (not beneath it).

Unlike standard body piercings, there are very few, if any, qualified professionals providing surgical implants and no state regulation of the practice. A qualified body piercer cannot one day decide to try putting implants into somebody; the techniques of body piercing and implanting are entirely different. Implants are a new and emerging type of body art, and still in a very experimental phase. Until this new frontier develops the kinds of operating procedures and professional standards typical of the body piercing community, implants are not recommended.

If someday you do decide to get an implant, be sure to go to a professional who works with surgical gloves and properly sterilized instruments in a sanitary environment. Like piercing, the major dangers of implants are infection and your body's rejection of, or allergy to, the jewelry.

Chapter 3

A Lifetime Commitment

T he decision to have a tattoo or body piercing is one that will be with you for the rest of your life, since tattoos and piercings are permanent, leaving at least a scar or hole. People's tastes often change with time. Fashion also changes. What happens if you get tired of your tattoo or piercing? What if tattoos and piercings become a fashion no-no ten years down the road? What if in a few years you find it difficult to get a job because of your tattoo or piercing or the scars and holes that remain after their removal?

Another consideration is that body modifications such as tattoos and piercings are considered to be unacceptable in certain situations. In the workplace, for instance, they are perceived as unprofessional by

While having gained acceptance in our culture, tattoos and piercings are still unacceptable in many workplaces.

many people. You shouldn't take your jewelry out every day for work because sometimes even older piercings can close up. So before getting pierced, you should ask your supervisor what the policy is on piercing. Rightly or wrongly, many employers believe that piercings and tattoos reflect on your work habits and reliability. They may also worry about how customers or clients will react to you. Just to be safe, ask your boss about company rules before you spend your money and risk your job on a tattoo or piercing.

What can you do if you become tired of having other people judge you as irresponsible or unprofessional because of your alternative fashion statement? There are ways to remove both tattoos and piercings, but your body will always bear their marks; no removal procedure will make your skin entirely smooth again. This is why it is extremely important to think about where you want to be in the future before you decide to receive a tattoo or piercing. These are permanent procedures that can never be fully undone.

Removing Piercings

Many people wrongly believe that if you remove the jewelry from a piercing, the opening will heal and close. This is untrue. Once properly healed, a piercing is usually permanent and, jewelry or no jewelry, you have a hole in your body. Facial and navel piercings tend to look unattractive without jewelry in them. While you can elect to stop wearing jewelry if you grow tired of your piercing, most of the time you will still have to live with a visible hole in your body.

Sometimes, a plastic surgeon can perform microsurgery to remove the original pierced tissue and, using an ultrafine suture, close the new wound. Plastic surgery can be quite expensive, however.

Removing Tattoos

While a tattoo is said to be forever, your love of it may not last nearly that long. Perhaps your tattoo job was botched by an amateur or a sloppy professional tattooist. Or maybe you no longer believe in the sentiment tattooed on your skin or are no longer in love with the person whose name is printed on your body. You may also be looking for a job and are worried about how your tattoo may hurt your chances. Don't worry; you're not alone. Some tattoo removal specialists estimate that half of all people who get a tattoo later regret it. The good news is that the latest laser removal techniques are more effective and have fewer side effects, such as scarring, than traditional methods. But laser removal is very expensive, takes several months, and may not make the tattoo entirely disappear. You will not walk in with a tattoo, receive one treatment, and walk out with no pain, no scar, and no sign of the tattoo. Unfortunately, the process is more complicated than that.

Tattoo removal used to be a painful, extreme experience that left scars and did not entirely remove the tattoo. Tattoos used to be sanded off the skin using acid, salt, or sandpaper, or cut off using a sharp scalpel. Lasers first began to be used for tattoo removal in the early 1980s, and they made the process far more effective and far less painful. The most common laser used was a CO_2 laser. A laser beam would be pointed at the tattooed area, scraping away the top layer of skin and exposing the second layer

Tattoo removal techniques using lasers were pioneered in the 1980s but caused burning and scarring.

where the tattoo was. The tattoo pigment was then removed with chemicals. The advantage of this type of laser was that tattoos were usually removed in one sitting. But because the laser beam was in continuous contact with the skin, there was often second-degree burning and scarring.

More recently, new removal procedures have been developed using "Q-Switching" lasers that release their beams in short, powerful bursts that do not harm the surface of the skin but do break up the tattoo pigment lying beneath the surface. There are three main types of Q-Switching lasers, each one working best on certain dye colors. Red, black, and blue tattoo pigments are the easiest to remove, orange and purple a little less so, while green and yellow are very difficult and may never fade completely. Most laser removal specialists say that complete tattoo removal is not possible. A good rule of thumb is that about 95 percent of a tattoo will fade if removed by a qualified laser removal specialist.

There are several other drawbacks to laser removal. On average, most patients require five to eight sessions, with at least four to six weeks between sessions. The procedure can be very expensive. Depending on how many visits you need to schedule, and on the size, type, and location of the tattoo, removal can cost anywhere from $500 to $2,000. Laser removal is rarely covered by medical insurance. While not nearly as painful as getting a tattoo, removal can hurt, too. The pain caused by the laser has been described as akin to being snapped with a thin rubber band or splattered with frying bacon grease. Side effects of laser removal are rare but can include either a lack or excess of skin color where the tattoo used to be, infection, scarring, and incomplete tattoo pigment removal.

The future for tattoo removal looks brighter. New techniques and better lasers are currently being developed that will remove more of the tattoo more quickly and less expensively. But chances are it will never become a cheap and easy procedure. Before you decide to get a tattoo, you should remind yourself that it is meant to be permanent and may not be possible to remove. Given the expense, pain, uncertainty, and waiting involved in laser removal—and the even worse removal alternatives—you should really spend some time thinking about tattooing and its risks before you get a tattoo. Then consider that the body art may be there forever, no matter what kind of social situation, romantic relationship, or job opportunity you may encounter in the future. The art you get today may not reflect where you are ten or twenty years from now.

Chapter 4

What You Should Know

If you have decided to get a tattoo or piercing and have thought about how much it costs, what image or jewelry you want, and where you want it, there may still be some obstacles in your way. There are some religious, legal, and health considerations that may prevent you from getting your tattoo or piercing.

Tattoos and piercings are considered taboo or unacceptable by many religions. Members of the Jewish faith and certain Christian denominations cannot be tattooed or pierced because of their religious beliefs. If your religion forbids these activities and you wish to remain in good standing, you cannot get a tattoo or piercing. Ask at your place of worship if tattoos and piercings are permitted in your religion.

If you are thinking about having a tattoo or piercing, you must also find out if it is legal to do so where you live. At the time this book was written, tattooing was illegal in Connecticut, Florida, Oklahoma, and South Carolina. Check with your state health department to find out if tattooing is legal in your community.

Regions that permit tattooing and body piercing may restrict these activities to persons eighteen years of age or older. Some communities may allow tattooing of those under eighteen only with the consent of a parent or guardian. In this case, your parent or guardian must go with you when you have the procedure performed, and both of you must bring some identification that proves your relationship. Again, contact the health department of your state to obtain information about such restrictions.

All of these laws exist to protect your health. Even if local laws permit you to get a tattoo or piercing, you may want to reconsider any plans you may have. The fact that so many health officials forbid these practices is strong evidence that they can put your health and your life in serious jeopardy.

In addition, there are several medical problems that make it dangerous to get a piercing or tattoo, such as diabetes, anemia, hemophilia, and other blood disorders. If you have one of these conditions, consult your doctor before receiving any tattoo or piercing.

How to Choose a Tattooist/Piercer

If you have decided to get a tattoo or piercing, your next important decision is where to get it done. Unfortunately, there is no formal training or certification required for piercers and tattooists. Almost anyone can legally set himself or herself up as a tattooist or piercer. The government only regulates the health standards of their shops, not their professional qualifications. So it is up to you to inspect the tattoo and piercing parlors beforehand and ask the right questions of the person who will perform the procedure.

You might start by talking to people you know who have received successful tattoos or piercings. Ask where they got them and if they were happy with the experience. Plan a visit to the shop, or several shops. Your tattooist/piercer should be working out of a legitimate place of business, not a seedy backroom or someone's basement. The shop should specialize only in tattooing or piercing; shops that double as hair salons or sell clothes, books, or music do not tend to employ the most experienced and professional piercers or tattooists. The shop should look as organized and smell as clean as a dentist's or doctor's office, and the piercing or tattooing should be done in a special separate room.

Don't be afraid to ask tattooists or piercers questions about their work. If they don't seem to want to answer you, go elsewhere. They should have a photo

A piercing or tattoo artist's space should be as sanitary as the office of a doctor or dentist.

Reputable tattooists and piercers have photo albums of their work available for new clients to look through.

album of their work to show you. Ask them how they sterilize their instruments and jewelry. Make sure that all supplies used during the procedure—gloves, jewelry, tools—are properly sterilized. All needles that are used must be brand-new and sterilized. Have them show you their autoclave and ask them when it was last tested (it should be tested once a month). Ask how they learned to pierce or tattoo and how long they have been doing it. You can also ask your local health department, which registers tattoo and piercing shops, for a recommendation. You may also check with the Better Business Bureau to see if any complaints have been filed against the shop you are considering.

Chapter 5

False Expectations

Many teenagers decide to get a tattoo or piercing before they are fully informed about the procedures and the results. They may be surprised by how much they have spent on a piercing or tattoo or by the pain involved in getting one. If they don't know how to properly care for their tattoo or piercing afterward, they may become disappointed by a tattoo that fades or a piercing that becomes infected and rejects the jewelry. All in all, without knowing the facts ahead of time, you are much more likely to be disappointed by your experience and by the end result.

Drawbacks of a Tattoo

Many people who are planning to get a tattoo are so excited that they neglect to think about what is involved in the procedure. Most simple tattoos take at least an hour to complete. Large or fancy tattoos take several hours or even several visits. The pain lasts throughout the procedure. It is not uncommon for a person to throw up or even faint. A responsible tattoo artist works only for three or four hours at one visit. A second visit is usually scheduled after the first section has had time to heal. Limiting the length of a tattoo procedure reduces the risk of illness.

In rare but serious cases, some very sensitive people have gone into shock while getting a tattoo. Because tattooing breaks the skin, you do put yourself at some risk for bloodborne infections such as HIV, hepatitis B and C, and tetanus. This is why it is crucial to make sure your tattooist is using properly sterilized needles and tools and is wearing surgical gloves. Without proper cleaning and protection from the sun, the tattoo may become infected or fade. Your tattooist should provide you with a sheet of "aftercare" instructions to prevent this (see chapter 6 for some care guidelines). You may also become allergic to one or more of the colored dyes used. If you are, your tattooist may have to "bleed" that color out and replace it with another.

Care of a Tattoo

Caring for your tattoo as advised by your tattoo artist will reduce the possibility of infection. It will also minimize fading of the colors. Still, all tattoos fade considerably as time passes. Black ink fades to a bluish gray. Other bright colors also become dull. This is normal.

Someone who is unhappy with a dull tattoo can arrange to have it touched up. More ink is applied to the tattoo, giving it a fresh appearance. But it is advisable to wait several years before having a tattoo touched up, and it should be done only a few times. You can get ink poisoning by having ink constantly reapplied to one area of the body. Ink poisoning is rare, but serious, and requires medical attention.

Unfortunately, India ink is sometimes used on a tattoo. This type of ink is very black and does not fade. Many people find this appealing. But you should never be tattooed with India ink. India ink contains poison. It probably will not kill you, but it can make you extremely ill. It can also prevent you from having children or cause birth defects in the children you do have. The type of poison in India ink affects the genes that you will pass on to your children, and flawed genes are a major cause of birth defects.

Drawbacks of Piercing

Piercing has some of the same drawbacks as tattooing. It can be intensely painful and fairly expensive. The charge for a piercing and one piece of jewelry ranges from $60 to $100. A fresh piercing also requires a great deal of care to prevent infection. The piercing and the area around it must be kept clean at all times.

The average healing time for a tattoo is four to six weeks, but a piercing may take much longer. Nose piercings can take four to six weeks to heal, while earlobes take six to eight weeks. Others, such as navel piercings, take four to six months. It should be noted that these estimates are just averages. People heal at different rates.

Until a piercing heals, it will feel tender and sensitive. Once it has healed, the discomfort should disappear. If a piercing is constantly itchy despite its being kept clean and dry, or if it is red and sore or oozing pus, it is probably infected. If you are not healing at all, or if you have signs of an infection, call a doctor immediately.

Specific problems with body piercing depend on the body part that is pierced. Piercings of the cartilage along the top of your ear heal more slowly than earlobe piercings because the tissue is different and the top of your ear is rubbed more during sleep. Tongue piercings swell a lot at first but heal quickly because the tongue has a large blood supply, which helps fight infection. Navel piercings get infected very easily because tight clothes don't allow enough air circulation and the area becomes damp. Using the

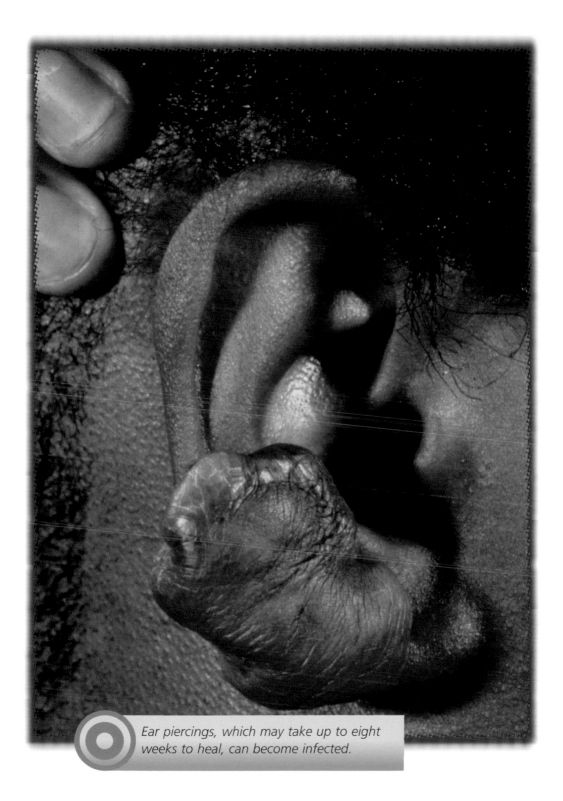

Ear piercings, which may take up to eight weeks to heal, can become infected.

wrong type of jewelry for your piercing can also lead to infection. If the jewelry is too thin or too heavy, your body may try to reject it. The area will swell, which is the body's way of trying to force the jewelry out. You may also develop an allergy to some of the metals in your jewelry.

For reasons unknown, some people's bodies are not suited to piercing. Their bodies literally reject piercings, even if they have been careful to follow the aftercare instructions provided by their piercer (see chapter 6 for some care guidelines). A severe infection develops, and the jewelry must be removed. The piercing then heals and closes, leaving a scar. This process is known as growing out or healing out. Some types of body piercings tend to grow out more often than others. For example, 50 percent of all navel piercings grow out. It is also possible that your body will accept one type of piercing and reject another. Your nose piercing may last, but your tongue piercing may close.

Chapter 6

Preventing Infection

We have already mentioned that you can be infected with hepatitis, HIV, or other diseases if you are tattooed or pierced with unsterilized equipment. You also know that an autoclave is used to sterilize tattooing and piercing equipment. If you decide, after considering all of the information, to have a piercing or tattoo, make certain that the equipment has been sterilized in an autoclave. You have the right to ask the person performing the procedure to use a new needle. A responsible practitioner will confirm the sterility of all equipment and will always use a new needle.

Another thing that you can do to protect your health is to make sure that the person performing the procedure is wearing latex gloves. This protects you

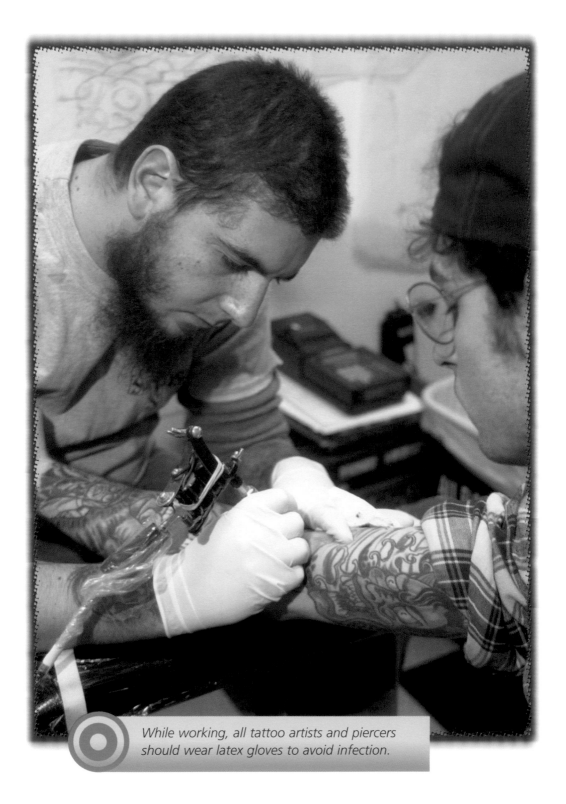

While working, all tattoo artists and piercers should wear latex gloves to avoid infection.

from infection by the practitioner and protects him or her from contracting any illness that you may have. Most tattooists and piercers routinely wear latex gloves whenever they perform their work. If your practitioner does not put on gloves, do not be afraid to ask him or her to do so. Your health is at stake!

Once you have a new tattoo or piercing, there are a number of things you can do to prevent infection and promote healing. The professional who performs the procedure should go over these instructions with you. It is essential that you follow them.

Infections frequently occur even with proper care. Improperly caring for a new tattoo or piercing is asking for trouble. Even minor infections can spread quickly and become serious. Some infections, such as gangrene, can be life threatening. If you develop an infection, seek medical attention immediately.

Avoiding Infection of a Tattoo

Tattooing makes your body vulnerable to infection. It is extremely important to keep a new tattoo bandaged for the first twenty-four hours. It is a fresh, open wound. Exposing a wound to the air means exposing it to limitless types of bacteria and other infection-causing agents. In order to avoid infecting the wound with germs, touch the area as little as possible and don't allow anyone else to touch it. An infection in a new tattoo is serious. It puts your health at risk.

An infection is also a risk to your tattoo. It is almost certain to damage the appearance of your new skin design. It may leave a scar, or it may make the colors of your tattoo uneven.

When the time comes to remove the bandage, first wet the gauze in the shower. Then wash the tattoo with antibacterial soap and water. Rinse the area thoroughly and pat it dry with a towel. Do not use alcohol or peroxide to clean the wound; they can dry a tattoo out. Apply an antibacterial ointment at least three times a day for two or three weeks. This will help the scab stay soft, preventing hardening and cracking. Always wash your hands to clean them of infection-causing germs before you apply the ointment. Never apply Vaseline or any other petroleum jelly to the wound. It seals the tattoo from the air, preventing it from healing. It can also seal in germs, causing an infection. Petroleum jelly also results in the formation of a heavy scab and a dull tattoo.

After you stop using the antibacterial ointment, continue to keep the scab moist with a cream-based, non-greasy skin lotion. Never pick or pull at the scabs on your tattoo. This will reopen the wound and increase your chances of an infection. Picking the scabs off can also cause permanent damage to the tattoo. On a new tattoo, the ink is very close to the surface of the skin. When you pick a scab, you are picking the ink out of your skin. When the scabs heal, the skin on your tattoo will be dry and will peel. Do not peel the dry skin off of your tattoo. Let nature take care of that. It is possible to reopen the wound this way, once again exposing you to infection.

Avoid exposure to direct sunlight for four weeks. Even just five minutes of direct sunlight on any part of a healing tattoo may cause an allergic reaction and may possibly fade the colors. It is always a good idea, whether tattooed or not, to use a strong, waterproof sunscreen when out in the sun.

Do not soak in a hot tub, take a hot bath, or go swimming until your peeling has stopped. Swimming or soaking in water will dry out your tattoo and prolong the healing process. And, since most swimming facilities are public, other people's germs may linger in the water and infect you. Whenever you get out of the shower, gently pat your tattoo dry with a clean towel. Then apply the antibacterial ointment or moisturizing lotion depending on where you are in the healing process.

Avoiding Infection of a Piercing

Like a tattoo, a piercing opens your body to infection because it involves the insertion of a foreign object into your skin, which your body may or may not accept. Consequently, your new piercing should be kept clean at all times. Always wash your hands with soap before touching or cleaning the pierced part during the healing process. Don't let anyone else touch the piercing during this period. At least three times a day, you should clean the pierced area with an antibacterial soap. Gently wash the area surrounding and including the piercing, being sure to remove all crusty formations from the piercing and jewelry. Rinse the area thoroughly of all soap, then pat it dry. The antibacterial soap should be enough to keep the area clean, but you may also apply an antibacterial ointment to the piercing. Prolonged use of ointments is not advisable, however, because they tend to keep the air away from the pierced area. After exercise, be sure to rinse the pierced area of all sweat. Sweat can irritate the piercing.

Some types of piercing require special care; ask your piercer for care instructions. Never use rubbing alcohol or hydrogen peroxide to clean your piercing; these may discolor some jewelry and will dry out your skin, preventing healing. Soaking your piercing in salt water can speed the healing process and loosen up crusty formations.

Always wear clean and loose-fitting clothing during healing. If you have a navel piercing, don't wear large belts, stockings, or bodysuits, and do not sleep on your stomach. Good air circulation is crucial for healing. Also be sure to change your bedsheets every week to avoid germs and bacteria. If your ear has been pierced, clean your telephone and sunglasses or eyeglasses with Lysol spray or rubbing alcohol. Wash the part of your glasses that touch your ear with soap and water. If your earlobe or ear cartilage has been pierced, avoid makeup and powders around your face and neck during the healing process.

Your flesh can heal onto the jewelry, which results in a painful and unattractive piercing. For that reason, you must turn the jewelry in your piercing at least three or four times a day. Wash your hands first, and then very gently turn the jewelry completely around five times. If your tongue or lip has been pierced, use a saltwater rinse or an antibacterial mouthwash that doesn't contain alcohol after every meal and snack.

Avoid public pools and hot tubs for two weeks after being pierced. The germs of other swimmers and bathers may stay in the water and infect you.

Remember that the healing process following a piercing can range from four weeks to six months or more. So anything you can do to speed up the process through careful aftercare is to your benefit.

Chapter 7

Alternatives to Tattooing and Piercing

Since tattoos and body piercings have become so fashionable, several products have become available that allow you to participate in the fad without actually getting a tattoo or a piercing.

Temporary tattoos, much like the ones you may have bought as a child, but greatly improved, have become extremely popular. A wide assortment of tattoo flash is available in temporary form. The colors of temporary tattoos have been greatly improved and are bright and vibrant. Temporary tattoos can be purchased in record stores and magazine shops everywhere. They are an inexpensive and safe alternative to permanent tattoos.

Henna painting, also known as mehndi, is a temporary form of body art that has as long and rich a

Mehndi and henna designs are fun and safe alternatives to permanently marking your body.

history as tattooing. It has become very popular with young people in North America recently, thanks largely to the pop star Madonna wearing henna designs in her videos and at public appearances. Henna painting is an art form traditionally associated with women and was often used to mark special events in a woman's life, such as marriage.

Henna painting is a painless, inexpensive procedure that involves the spreading of an olive-green paste made from leaves of the henna plant on the body in whatever design or pattern you choose. After about an hour, the paste dries and is brushed off the skin, revealing your design in a light orange color. This will darken after a few days to a deep brown.

In North America, henna painting is sometimes called a "temporary tattoo," but it should not be confused with adhesive tattoos. Some people who want to get a tattoo but are nervous about the results use henna painting to test out the pattern they think they want tattooed on their body. It's a risk-free trial run. If the pattern is disappointing, it will disappear in a couple of weeks with none of the pain or expense associated with tattoo removal. Also, with henna painting, you can treat your body as if it were an erasable canvas, and sport a brand-new design every few weeks.

Body jewelry for nonpierced people is becoming extremely popular. Clip-on earrings, nose rings, and

You should think about all of the possible consequences of having a tattoo or piercing before you actually get one.

navel rings are widely available. Magnetic studs—which look like a piercing but are held together by the attraction of two magnets—are also available for the ears, lips, nose, or tongue. This jewelry costs less than a piercing, and it gives you the opportunity to be part of the piercing trend without having to make any holes in your body and risk infection or scarring.

The current fascination with tattoos and body piercing has caused many people to consider getting a tattoo or piercing. It is important to think about all the possible consequences before actually getting one: the possibility of contracting a bloodborne disease, such as AIDS; the possibility of infection; the possibility that your body will reject a piercing, leaving a hole or scar; the possibility that, when fashions change, you may wish to get rid of a piercing or tattoo; the possibility that a piercing or tattoo will negatively affect your future; and the fact that removing a tattoo or piercing is expensive.

If, after carefully considering all of the information, you do decide to have a body piercing or a tattoo done, do so with care, for the sake of your health. If you decide that piercing and tattooing are not for you, there are many fashion alternatives available that do not involve the puncturing of your skin and the permanent marking of your body.

It is your body. It is up to you to take care of it wisely.

Glossary

autoclave Machine that sterilizes tattoo, piercing, and surgical equipment by using steam pressure.

flash Selection of tattoo designs that hangs on the walls of tattoo parlors.

gangrene The death of soft tissues due to loss of blood supply.

hepatitis Acute viral disease involving inflammation of the liver.

hygiene Cleanliness; practices to conserve health.

rite of passage Ceremony or event that celebrates an important event in a person's life.

septum The part of the nose that separates the two nostrils.

syphilis A bloodborne disease that can't be
completely cured.

tetanus An infectious disease usually caused by
an open wound that can lead to lockjaw.

tuberculosis An infectious and potentially fatal
disease of the lungs.

Where to Go for Help

In the United States

Alliance of Professional Tattooists
428 Fourth Street, Unit 3
Annapolis, MD 21403
(410) 216-9630
Web site: http://www.safetattoos.com

American Society for Dermatologic Surgery (ASDS)
9930 Meacham Road
Schaumburg, IL 60173-6016
(800) 441-2737
Web site: http://www.asds-net.org
The ASDS also publishes fact sheets on dermatologic
surgery for tattoo removal and microsurgery.

Association of Professional Piercers
PMB 286
5446 Peachtree Industrial Boulevard
Chamblee, GA 30341
(888) 555-4APP (4277)
Web site: http://www.safepiercing.org

In the United States, your state health department
is another great resource for information on the
dangers of tattooing and body piercing. Look
in the white pages of your telephone book for
the address and phone number.

In Canada

Health Canada
A.L. 0904A
Ottawa, ON K1A 0K9
(613) 957-2991
Web site: http://www.hc-sc.gc.ca

See a dermatologist if you have questions about the
safety of tattooing or body piercing, or if you have
a problem with a tattoo or piercing. See a cosmetic
surgeon if you have questions about removing a
tattoo or piercing.

Web Sites

General information on tattooing, flash collections, tattoo parlor directories, articles, and bookstores:

Alliance of Professional Tattooists
http://www.safetattoos.com

Sites that contain information on tattooing, piercing, body modifications, health, and safety:

Tat2duck.Com
http://www.angelfire.com/ct/Tat2Duck/index.html

Tattoodocs.Com
http://www.tattoodocs.com

Information on tattoo removal:
Marshall Brain's How Stuff Works
http://www.howstuffworks.com/tattoo-removal.html

For Further Reading

Bish, Barry. *Body Art Chic: The First Step-by-Step Guide to Body Painting, Temporary Tattoos, Piercing, Hair Designs, Nail Art.* North Pomfret, VT: Trafalgar Square Publishing, 1999.

Camphausen, Rufus C. *Return of the Tribal: A Celebration of Body Adornment.* Rochester, VT: Park Street Press, 1997.

Graves, Bonnie B. *Tattooing and Body Piercing.* Mankato, MN: LifeMatters, 2000.

Kaplan, Leslie S. *Coping with Peer Pressure.* Rev. ed. New York: The Rosen Publishing Group, Inc., 1999.

Krakow, Amy. *The Total Tattoo Book.* New York: Warner Books, 1994.

Miller, Jean-Chris. *The Body Art Book: A Complete, Illustrated Guide to Tattoos, Piercings, and Other Body Modifications*. New York: The Berkeley Publishing Group, 1997.

Taylor, Barbara. *Everything You Need to Know About AIDS*. Rev. ed. New York: The Rosen Publishing Group, Inc., 1998.

Weiss, Stefanie Iris. *Everything You Need to Know About Mehndi, Temporary Tattoos, and Other Temporary Body Art*. New York: The Rosen Publishing Group, Inc., 2000.

Index

Index

About the Author

Laura Reybold is a freelance writer who lives and works in New York.

Photo Credits

Cover © Yellow Dog Productions/Imagebank; p. 2 © The Image Works; p. 8 © Everett Collection/Robert Hepler; pp. 13, 21, 22, 35, 36, 44, 53 by Maura Boruchow; p. 15 © Charles and Josette Lenars/Corbis; p. 19 © Alan Becker/Imagebank; p. 26 © David Paul Productions/Imagebank; pp. 29, 41 © Custom Medical; p. 51 © John Eastcott/Yva Momatiuk/The Image Works.

Layout

Thomas Forget